F*CK YOU
WATCH ME

ELAINE BREWER

F*ck You, Watch Me

What Do We Have Here?

*F*ck You, Watch Me is a raw, unfiltered blend of storytelling, soul work, and straight-up truth. Part memoir, part rally cry, it's my reckoning with the life I built and the lies I told myself to survive it.

For years, I helped others heal. As a coach, I could walk people out of the fire, hold space, and ask the questions that sparked transformation. But behind closed doors? I was the one unraveling.

This is what happens when the coach finally takes her own damn advice. You're eavesdropping as I navigate the wreckage—no script, no filter. Just honesty, grit, and the kind of truth that splits you wide open.

Through real-time journal entries, I rip the mask off and expose it all. It's not polished. It's not perfect. But it's mine—and it's the story of how I rose, one gut-wrenching, honest step at a time.

These aren't reflections. They're revelations.
This isn't a guidebook. It's a survival story. A reckoning. A voice for the ones still suffering in silence.

I didn't write this book because I wanted to.
I wrote it because freedom demanded it.
Because silence was a slow death. Because the mask became a cage. Because pretending almost destroyed me.

So, if you're done hiding, done shrinking,
done carrying what was never yours to hold—
Let's walk through this fucking fire together

Acknowledgments

To my boys—
Thank you for loving me, believing in me, and always
knowing what I was capable of. But most of all, thank
you for seeing *her* in me—even when I couldn't. You
never stopped believing she was still in there.
I'm back now, and I'm never letting go again.
Thank you for being my *Why*.

Born to be Wild

I've always known I was born to raise hell.

Even as a kid, I wasn't drawn to fairy tales or soft-spoken role models. I worshiped the wild ones, the women who couldn't be boxed in, who radiated raw power, who burned too bright to be dimmed.

Stevie Nicks, cloaked in mystery and divine feminine chaos.

Princess Diana, tender yet rebellious, and quietly shook empires.

Alanis Morissette, belting rage and truth like sacred hymns.

Juliette Lewis, gloriously unhinged, magnetic, and wild to the core.

Idgie Threadgoode, the poker-playing, bee-charming tomboy who stood up for love and justice in *Fried Green Tomatoes*.

Penny Lane, who didn't just live the vibe—she *was* the vibe.

Angelina Jolie's Lisa Rowe in *Girl, Interrupted*, cracking the system wide open with madness, brilliance, and truth.

Beth Dutton—my spirit animal in cowboy boots, setting fire to everything that dared to hold her back.

These women weren't just characters or icons.

They were hurricanes.

They didn't survive the fire.

They *were* the fire.

And for a while, it looked like I was one of them. Bold. Untamed. Loud. A risk-taker. But underneath the bravado, I was shackled— tightly bound by invisible chains forged from trauma, guilt, and fear. I lived with the exhausting belief that I was simultaneously too much and never enough. My mind was a battlefield, my spirit held hostage, and my body kept the score.

I wanted to be wild. But first, I had to survive.

I won't drag you through every chapter of my childhood or every early bruise on my spirit. What matters are the moments that slowly dimmed my fire—moments that turned my roar into a whisper. The following experiences are the ones that I know made an imprint and put me on a path to the Undoing of Me.

The Undoing

Am "I" Wrong?

As a child, I was wild, curious, social, and full of life. It was the 90s, and back then, there wasn't much compassion for kids like me. Learning disabilities and ADD weren't seen as different ways of thinking— they were seen as problems to fix. I couldn't read well. Math felt like a foreign language. My attention darted in a hundred directions. So, they gave me Ritalin.

It was a chemical straightjacket. It killed my appetite. It took a social butterfly and made her feel numb and isolated. But the worst part? The crash. Imagine a little girl, too young to understand what brain-altering drugs even are, absolutely spiraling from the comedown. The rage. The outbursts. Flipping tables and screaming into the void.

I was too much, and no one really knew what to do with me.

At school, they put me in "resource." In the 90s, that word wasn't gentle; it came loaded with shame. I was placed in a classroom with kids who had severe mental and physical disabilities—some couldn't speak, some needed feeding tubes, and many were wheelchair-bound or required full-time aides. And there I sat, looking around, trying to make sense of it.
Was something wrong with me? Was I handicapped? Was I incapable or just... stupid?

That was the moment—the first mental blow.
Something is wrong with me.
And that thought stayed lodged in my chest for years to come.

I kept it secret. I became the chameleon. I'd hide in the bathroom before the bell rang so no one would see me walk into the "special class." I learned to mask early—to pretend, to adapt, and to blend in. I was terrified anyone would find out the truth: that I was different. That I struggled. That I didn't fit the mold. I carried shame for being curious, energetic, and uninterested in school, but fascinated with the world around me, and these were the very things that made me, *Me*.

That's how it starts, sometimes. Not with a single act of violence or abandonment, but with a quiet, devastating message:
You are wrong for how you are wired.

And when you believe that long enough, it changes you. It disconnects you from your own magic.

The Betrayal

At 18, I thought I was in love. Three years into a relationship with the guy I thought was my forever, I found out he'd been sleeping with one of my best friends. And it wasn't some one-time lapse in judgment—it was a choice they kept making, over and over again. But the real gut punch? Most of my circle of friends knew and said nothing. The ones I laughed with, cried with, trusted with my most vulnerable self… stood by in silence while I played the fool.

That was the moment the walls went up. The betrayal cut so deep, I swore I'd never let anyone that close again. That was the day I stopped trusting freely, and I've struggled to build real friendships ever since.

After that, I started drinking. Not casually. Not socially. I drank alone. I drank to disappear. To dull the ache. To sleep without nightmares.

That's when my brain learned its first toxic mantra: ***Ahhh... alcohol helps.***

I Didn't Train for This

A year later, I reconnected with a guy I knew from high school. He was back in town visiting family after a deployment to Iraq. Now, he was a Navy EOD tech—his job was to disarm bombs for a living. Quiet. Grounded. Sharp. He had a stillness that made you lean in. He felt safe and dangerous, all at once.

I fell fast. Headfirst. Heart open.

He wasn't looking for anything serious, but I didn't care. I bartended just to afford flights to Virginia Beach to be with him for a weekend. I squeezed my way into his world, determined to matter. Determined to be the one who stuck.

Soon, He would be deploying again—this time with a SEAL Team. I knew if I didn't lock it down, I'd lose him. To someone easier. Prettier. Less... complicated.

I wasn't the smartest, the skinniest, or the prettiest girl. But I had fire. Grit. A relentless drive to be chosen.

And I was. Three years later, he asked me to move in. We made a home in California, got a German shepherd named Nikko, our first "baby," and started building a life. For the first time, it felt like peace.

One day in Monterey, he dropped to one knee. I said yes. To him. To stability. To belonging.

Then the phone rang.

An invitation to screen for SEAL Team 6. The best of the best. The most elite fighting force in the world.

And everything shifted again.

We were back in Virginia Beach. Far from family, far from help. At 25, I became a mother. Six weeks after our son was born, He deployed. I was terrified and alone with a newborn. I didn't train for this…

When he wasn't deployed, he was training, doing work-ups, or held up at work. The command tempo was unrelenting. The distance between us widened.

I wore every hat: mom, dad, chef, dogwalker, housekeeper, cheerleader, appointment keeper. I was dying under the weight of responsibility. I was trying to survive, and in that desperation, I disappeared.

Un-Comfortably Numb

Then came August 6, 2011.

A Chinook helicopter was shot down in Wardak Province, Afghanistan. Thirty teammates. One military working dog. **No survivors.**

That night, we were at a teammate's welcome-home party. My Husband's pager went off. An all-call. Everyone to the command.

I thought he was being deployed—again. I panicked. I was drinking, spiraling. A friend gave me a Tylenol PM. I passed out cold.

But he wasn't leaving on a mission. He was going to deliver the worst news imaginable: Nick, one of his closest friends, had been killed in the crash.

Before he left to notify Nick's wife and kids, He came home. He needed to be held. To breathe. But I was unconscious. Unavailable. Gone.

When I woke the next morning, devastation was everywhere—and I hadn't been there when he needed me most.

That was the day shame took root in my body. And it never let go.

After that, the funerals kept coming. We drank to honor the dead. To suppress the fear. To numb so we could survive the pain and erase the stark realization that we were not invincible.

But I was unraveling.

Being part of "The Command" came with unspoken expectations. These men were warriors. And the wives? We were expected to be just as tough, poised, polished, and perfect.

So, I performed. Land Rover? Check. Boob job? Check. Fitness instructor? Check. Full face of makeup at Target? Always.

But it was all a costume, a facade.

What people didn't see was the quiet destruction going on behind closed doors. The SEAL Teams and this team in particular were a constant barrage of death, deployments, and divorces. It was a persistent reminder that no one gets out of this unscathed.

My husband kept deploying, year after year. And each time he came home, he was a little more hollow. A little less *him*.

And me? I had given up everything. My career. My passions. My identity.

I had completely lost myself. I was a shell of a woman.

I was just duct tape. And I was starting to peel off.

The drinking got worse. The anxiety constricted. Depression settled like a heavy fog. Suicidal thoughts didn't scare me—they felt like an escape hatch.

I became paranoid. That he'd die. That he'd cheat. That we'd fall apart.

I couldn't sleep. I'd get up in the middle of the night to clean. Obsessively. Because if *that* knock ever came—if someone came to tell me he wasn't coming home—my house had to be spotless.

It was the last shred of control I had…

I wish I could say that once he retired, life calmed down and I finally got my shit together, but that would be a lie. Life kept coming. We welcomed our second son, and he was anything but easy—colicky, restless, constantly needing to be held. It wasn't until he turned two that we discovered he had Autism. Then came COVID, and the world lost its damn mind. The chaos didn't let up. The hits just kept coming. It would be years before I finally hit my breaking point.

What Now?

Since I turned 18, it felt like life just kept coming for me. One trauma hit after another. I never had time to process or recover, just survive the next blow. I was exhausted, stuck in survival mode, and losing parts of myself along the way.

Eventually, I didn't know who I was. Not as a woman. Not as a mother. Not as a wife, not as anything.

The fire? Gone.
The fight? Fading.
Elaine—the wild, relentless, spitfire version of me—had vanished.

So, what now?

What do you do when your fire burns out and all that's left is smoke?

Do you wait? Do you grieve? Do You Give Up?

This was the undoing.

And the beginning of the rise I didn't see coming.

What you'll find here is a compilation of some of my journal entries, thoughts, and insights from my first 100 days of sobriety.

These pages hold my truth, my inspiration, and the roadmap back to myself. I don't share this because I have it all figured out—I share it as a humble warrior, hoping it might reach someone else who feels lost and is trying to find their way home.

This is the raw, real journey of Unfucking myself and the rise of the woman I was always meant to be.

The Wisdom

Use It, or Don't.

I'm not your guru, and this isn't a manual. This ain't 12 Step, babe—it's just my truth. Pulled from the wreckage, written in real-time, stitched together with raw honesty. If it speaks to you, hell yeah—take it and run. If it doesn't, leave it. Burn it. Keep moving. I'm not here to fix you. I'm just showing you what helped me crawl out, in case it helps you do the same.

Freedom Isn't Free

Freedom Isn't Free. Not in War, and Not in Recovery.

In the military, they say freedom isn't free.
It's bought with blood, sweat, discipline, and sacrifice.
The same holds true for sobriety.

Recovery is a battlefield of its own.
You're not just walking away from a substance; you're declaring war on the parts of you that found comfort in chaos.
You're shedding the armor that no longer serves you, and standing exposed in your truth.

You don't get to "just be free."
You earn it.
With every early morning, you rise when your body wants to quit.
With every party you walk out of.

With every emotion, you sit with instead of being numb.
With every temptation you face and say, Not today. I've fought too hard for this.

Freedom is the reward for discipline.
For consistency when it's boring.
For honesty when it's uncomfortable.
For sacrifice when no one is watching.

And here's the miracle…
The longer you fight for your freedom, the more it becomes who you are.
Not a punishment. Not a sentence.
A gift.
A power.
A return to who you were always meant to be.

So, if you're tired, good.
That means you're in the fight.
And if you're still standing, damn right you are. Because freedom isn't free.
But you?
You're proving you're worth the price!

Reflection Prompt:

Today marks the beginning of your fight.

Freedom isn't something you just wake up with.
It's something you *earn*.
Through discomfort. Through honesty. Through choosing growth over escape, one hard decision at a time.

So, let's begin with this:

What does *freedom* mean to you *right now*?

What are you walking away from, and what are you walking toward?

What are you willing to sacrifice to reclaim your peace, your power, your life?

Who are you choosing to become, and what does that version of you stand for?

For My Boys

I'm doing this because my boys deserve the clearest, strongest, most grounded version of their mom.
Because their laughter, their safety, their joy, it means more to me than any buzz, any escape, any moment of relief.

I choose to feel it all. The stress, the overwhelm, the anxiety, without checking out.
Because being here, really here, matters more than numbing ever did.

I'm building something bigger than a sober day—I'm building a legacy of resilience.
I'm showing my sons what courage looks like.
That when life feels heavy, I don't run; I rise.

This isn't just about giving up a drink.
It's about giving them the best of me.
The version with clear eyes at bedtime.
The deep breath when I'd rather scream.
The arms that hold them tight, with a mind that's fully present.

I'm not doing this just for me.
I'm doing it for them, for us.
And that's a gift that we will all carry forever.

Reflection Prompt:

What's your *why*?

Who or what is worth showing up for, clear, strong, and fully present?
What legacy are you building with the choices you make today?

Think about the people you love, the life you want, the version of yourself you're becoming.
When the urge to check out creeps in, what brings you back?
Write it down.
Claim it.
Because knowing your *why* gives your journey purpose and power.

The Storm Is Necessary

Not every storm comes to destroy you.

Some come to cleanse you.

We like to chase the sunny days. The light. The warmth. The feeling of safety. But the truth is, if life were always bright and easy, we'd never know our own strength. Sometimes, we need the storm. We need to be struck by lightning; jolted out of our numb autopilot.

We need to be shaken by thunder to remember what it feels like to be alive. We need to be drenched by rain to rinse off the illusions, the expectations, the lies we've told ourselves. Because it's only when we're pounded down by life that we discover what we're really made of.

Will we drown in the flood, or will we plant our feet, root down, and bloom? The storm is not your punishment; it's your invitation.

To rise. To grow. To evolve. To stop pretending and start becoming.

You don't just survive the storm; you become something new because of it.

Reflection Prompt:

What storm once felt like total destruction, but in hindsight, cleared the path for something better?

How did it reshape you? What false beliefs or attachments did it strip away?

If you're in a storm now, what lesson might it be bringing?

And when the thunder rumbles and everything feels uncertain, will you hide from it, or rise with it and learn to dance in the rain?

"Just Do Nothing"

Funny how the hardest thing in sobriety can be doing nothing.

It takes way more effort to relapse: go get the drink, pour it, hide it, pretend you're fine, deal with the shame spiral after. That's exhausting.

But in early sobriety, doing nothing felt impossible. I had to stay constantly busy just to avoid doing that.

Then came the next layer of work: learning how to be still. To be bored. To sit with the itch without scratching it.

Turns out, "doing nothing" is a skill, just like regulating your nervous system, communicating your needs, or building a real connection. It's uncomfortable at first. But it's powerful.

So today, don't pick it up. Don't buy it. Don't pour it.
Just do Nothing.

Reflection Prompt:

When was the last time you *let yourself* do nothing?
No distraction. No fix. No escape. Just presence.

What emotions or sensations come up when you're still?
Can you sit with them without numbing, fixing, or fleeing?

What might you discover if you stop trying to outrun the discomfort—and just *let it pass*?

Spirits

They call alcohol a spirit for a reason.

It starts as ease.
Takes the edge off.
Makes the room lighter.
Feels like connection.

But alcohol doesn't just take; it trades.
Clarity for calm.
Memory for quiet.
Purpose for escape.

It promises peace
while quietly stealing it.

And sip by sip,
You're the one being poured out.

What was once a spirit drawn from the essence of the mash becomes
a spirit that extracts the essence of your soul.

Reflection Prompt:

They call it a spirit for a reason, because it doesn't just take, it trades.

    What did alcohol offer you in the beginning?
    What did it *really* cost you over time?
    What did it make you trade?
    What parts of yourself did it slowly extract?

Now ask yourself:
What are you ready to reclaim and how will you begin to fill back up?

Feeling, Thought, Behavior

I'm reading a book called 'Why Has Nobody Told Me This Before' and it talks about how we make decisions. I broke it down in case it helps someone else.

Here's how it goes:
1.   A feeling hits.
Out of nowhere, you feel off. Anxious. Lonely. Frustrated. Your chest gets tight, your thoughts race.
You don't even know why, you just know it doesn't feel good & you want out.
2.   Then the thoughts start.
"I can't deal with this." "Nothing's getting better."
They are often just echoes of old pain trying to make sense of the emotion.
3.   Then the action follows.
You check out. You grab a drink—it's just a pattern. One that used to help us cope.

Your brain is trying to make sense of what you're feeling by connecting it to something it already knows, like it's pulling a file from the cabinet labeled "What do we do when we feel this way?"

If most of your past experiences involved thinking "f*ck it" & reaching for a drink to self-soothe, that becomes the default response. It's the path your brain knows best; you've created a superhighway to that action & response.

We need to build a new path. At first, it'll feel like a bumpy, unpaved dirt road. It's unfamiliar, uncomfortable, maybe even awkward. But the more you choose a new thought & take a different action, the path gets stronger. Over time, that becomes the new superhighway & the urge to drink becomes the unpaved dirt road.

And that, friends, is neuroplasticity in action. Your brain can rewire. You just have to keep choosing the new road.

Learning how to break the cycle.
- Start by naming the feeling. "This is anxiety."
Call it out. It loses power when it's seen.
- Question the thought. "Is this really true?"
Remind yourself: thoughts aren't facts.
- Change the action.
Move your body. Step outside. Text someone. Do one thing that supports who you're becoming, not who you were.

This is the new way forward:
Name the emotion.
Challenge the thought.
Create a new action.

Reflection Prompt:

Can you recall a moment recently when a feeling took over and led you down an old, familiar path?
What was the feeling? What thought followed? What action did you take?

Now flip it:
What might have changed if you had named the emotion, challenged the thought, and chosen a different action?

What's one healthy behavior, no matter how small, you can practice the next time that feeling shows up?
Is there a new hobby or routine that could help you build that new path, step by step?

God, the Universe, and a Prayer

I'm not a religious person. I don't go to church or talk to God like He is always listening. But I knew I needed something bigger than me. I had tried doing it on my own and failed more times than I could count.

So, one night, I just prayed.
Nothing fancy.
No script.
Just: *"I'll do my part. I'll carry the weight, show up, do the hard work. But please—I need you to take away the desire. Take away the grip alcohol has on me."*

And then the wildest thing happened.
He did.

The cravings lessened. The strength came. And I kept my end of the deal. I stayed in it. I kept showing up. And once I did, the real miracles started to unfold. It was like the Universe started working on my behalf. Opportunities, connections, ideas; they just kept showing up.

I remember telling my husband, "It's so weird. Every time I stop drinking, life stops happening *to* me and starts happening *for* me."

Maybe it was always happening for me.
Maybe I was just too numb, too foggy, too tuned out to see it.

But now I do.
I see the blessings everywhere. The timing. The people. The shifts. It feels like God is leaving me a trail of breadcrumbs, showing me I'm on the right path.

They say you find God when you've got nowhere else to turn.
And in that quiet moment of asking for help, everything began to shift.
Not because I handed over my power,
But because I stopped trying to hold it all by myself.

Reflection Prompt:

Are you open to the idea that something greater *wants* to help you, but you have to be willing to receive it?

What signs or "breadcrumbs" might already be guiding you, if you slowed down enough to notice?

What do you believe about God or spirituality? How can this help you on this journey?

Don't Avoid the Mirror

Lately, I've learned that when I get triggered, angry, or overly judgmental, it's often not about the other person—it's about me. They're holding up a mirror, reflecting something I haven't wanted to face. Instead of reacting, I've started asking: *What is this bringing up in me?*

Of course, I still react, I'm human. But more and more, I catch myself and choose reflection over reactivity.

A woman on the Reframe app recently posted about a baby shower she attended in early sobriety. She was venting about how the whole event centered around champagne and cocktails. She even mentioned the pregnant mom having a few sips, and was clearly upset and shaming everyone involved.

Instead of piling it on or defending the drinking, I asked her: *What if this is a mirror?* I shared a bit about how our reactions often come from unresolved parts of ourselves.

She replied later and said, "You're right. My husband was always afraid I wouldn't be able to stop drinking while pregnant. That fear still haunts me."

That was it. Her judgment wasn't really about those women—it was about her own past, her own fear.

That's what mirrors do; they show us what we haven't healed yet.

So, the next time someone triggers you, pause. Don't avoid the mirror. Look into it. There's a lesson waiting.

Reflection Prompt:

Think back to a time when you were triggered by someone: angry, judgmental, or reactive.

What was it *really* about?

Was there an unresolved fear, shame, or wound being reflected back at you?

Now ask yourself:

Can you see that person or situation differently now?

What would it feel like to respond with curiosity instead of judgment?

What healing might be possible if you stopped avoiding the mirror and started listening to what it's trying to show you?

Why "Just One" is so hard.

That first drink?
It immediately starts messing with your brain's control center, your Executive Functioning and Inhibitory Control.

That's the part of your brain that helps you:
- Pause before reacting
- Make smart choices
- Stick to your plan
- Stay aware of what the hell you're doing

Once alcohol hits your system, that part starts going offline. Which means the voice that tells you to stop?
It's already losing power after drink #1.

That's why moderation doesn't work for a lot of us.
Because the ability to moderate is the first thing alcohol takes away.

And if you're someone who's dealt with trauma, ADHD, anxiety, or chronic stress?
Your executive functioning is already running on overdrive.
Add alcohol—and you've just flipped the off switch for your internal brakes and moderation control.

It's not about weakness. It's chemistry.

It's about neurobiology.
It's about understanding how alcohol affects your brain, and being honest about what's actually happening, not what you *wish* would happen when you "just have one."

Reflection Prompt:

Have you ever told yourself, *"Just one,"* only to spiral into more?

What actually happens in your mind and body after that first drink? Be honest. Not what you *hope* will happen, but what *usually* does.

How does alcohol affect your ability to stay in control, make decisions, or follow through on what you promised yourself?

Left Behind

Yesterday, my husband drove our son to hockey camp in Ohio.
He packed up, hugged me, and left.
I was alone in the house—a rare, quiet moment.

But my body didn't feel peaceful.
It felt… threatened.

Not because I was unsafe, but because I was alone—and not by
choice. That stirred a trigger I've come to recognize more clearly in
sobriety: When someone leaves—even for something as normal as
a road trip—my nervous system flinches like it's being abandoned.

There's a wound there.
A belief etched into me after years of being left to hold everything
together alone.
Years of deployments. Nights filled with worry. Weeks of silence.
Birthday parties and holidays with one parent missing.
Every time, I stayed behind, holding the household, holding the
pain, pretending I wasn't afraid.

But I *was* afraid.
Afraid he wouldn't come back.
Afraid something would happen, and I wouldn't be enough to carry
it all.
Afraid of being forgotten. Replaced.
Afraid that everyone I love eventually leaves.

Over time, those moments stopped being isolated incidents and hardened into beliefs:
"People leave."
"I'm not enough for them to stay."
"Being alone means being abandoned."

So now, even years later, even when the separation is small and safe, my body still interprets it as loss.
That's why being alone *by choice* feels fine. Restorative, even.
Because I'm in control. Because no one left me.

But when someone leaves, and I didn't choose it?
It doesn't feel like absence.
It feels like loneliness.
And underneath that loneliness is something more primal: Fear.

Before, I would drink the second that pain surfaced.
Not to celebrate, but to numb what waited beneath the stillness.

But sobriety doesn't give me that option.
I have to face what's here.
And what's here is a scared version of me who still believes people don't stay.
Who still thinks she has to prove she can survive without anyone.
Who fears the people she loves will either leave or be taken.

These aren't irrational fears. These triggers were earned.
A Husband who came back changed. Teammates who never came home.
Boyfriends who cheated. Friends who disappeared.
The mind remembers. And the body keeps the score.

But here's the shift:
Sobriety doesn't just take away the alcohol.
It gives us space.
To pause instead of react.
To observe instead of escape.
To ask:

"What am I really afraid of right now?"
"Is this pain present or is the past trying to replay itself?"
"What if I believed I was still safe, even when people leave?"
"What if I'm not actually being left behind?"

In that pause, we get to rewire the nervous system.
We get to choose a new response.
To anchor.
To ground.
To remind ourselves:
We are safe and secure.

Curiosity creates new wiring. Reflection replaces autopilot. In this space, we get to meet ourselves with grace, awareness, and self-compassion.

Reflection Prompt:

Think about a recent moment when you felt triggered, especially by something that seemed small or insignificant.

What was the situation?

What emotion came up first?

When have you felt that way before?

Is the intensity of the trigger coming from the *present moment*, or an *old wound* being reactivated?

What might your body be trying to protect you from?

What would it look like to respond with curiosity instead of automatic reactivity?

Triggers aren't signs that you're broken.
They're invitations to listen, to feel, and to heal what's still asking for your attention.

Don't give the devil a seat at your table.

That urge to escape, that whisper saying "just one won't hurt," don't mistake it for your own voice.
It's the enemy, trying to sabotage your comeback story.

You've fought too damn hard to get here.
Your mind, your body, your peace, they're sacred ground now.

Don't let the devil dine where healing is happening.

Guard it.
Fight it.
And if the devil shows up thirsty & hungry, remind him, this table's full.

Only healing, strength, and truth are served here.

Reflection Prompt:

Who or what is trying to steal a seat at your table right now? Is it temptation? Shame? Self-doubt?
Name it.
Then ask yourself: *Does this thought deserve a voice in my healing?*
What would it look like to guard your peace like sacred ground today?
What truth do you need to speak to the lies trying to sneak in?

It's the Climb

Sobriety is my Everest.
Not because it's glamorous. Not because it's easy.
But because it asks everything of me.
Every step forward feels like it shouldn't be possible.
And still, I climb.

Some days, the air is thin.
Some days, I stumble, I ache, I want to turn back.
But this mountain has carved me into something stronger.
Not despite the struggle, but because of it.

I don't climb for applause.
I don't chase the peak for the view.
I climb because there's no going back.
Because I'm becoming someone I've never been before—
Clear. Present. Unshakable.

Reflection Prompt:

What mountain are *you* climbing?

It doesn't have to be sobriety. Maybe it's healing. Grief. Starting over.
Finding yourself again.
Whatever it is, it's your climb. And it's shaping you.

What has the struggle taught you so far?
Where have you stumbled, and where have you surprised yourself
with your strength?

You don't have to be at the summit to be proud of the climb.
Reflect on how far you've come, and who you're becoming with
every step.

The Cosmic Jackpot

Neil DeGrasse Tyson says that if you were born human, you've won the Cosmic Jackpot.

You were born on a living, breathing miracle.

Out of the endless void of space, Earth is the only known place with life. And not just any life, oceans that sing, forests that dance, skies that burn pink at sunset.
And from all that beauty, you emerged.

The atoms in your body were forged in ancient stars.
The oxygen in your lungs came from trees.
The blood in your veins flows with the memory of rivers.

You are not separate from this planet.
You are Earth, thinking, feeling, walking around in awe of itself.
-Neil DeGrasse Tyson

Remember:
The same miracle that created mountains and monarch butterflies...
created you.

Treat yourself and this planet like the once-in-a-universe master-piece that it is.

Your chances of becoming a life on Earth are 1 in 400 trillion.
You've won the Cosmic Jackpot!

Reflection Prompt:

What does it mean to *truly* realize that you are a once-in-a-universe miracle?

How would your choices about your body, your relationships, and your healing change if you *really believed* you were made of stardust?

Write about a moment when you felt connected to something bigger than yourself.
Did it humble you? Empower you? Both?

And now ask yourself:
Are you living like you won the Cosmic Jackpot?
What would it look like if you did?

Even Though — I Will.

This became my mantra.
It's inspired by Psalm 23:4:
"Even though I walk through the valley of the shadow of death, I will fear no evil."

Whether you're religious or not, these words are a war cry—a declaration of strength.

Even though it's hard, I will keep fighting.
Even though I want a drink, I will stay present.
Even though I'm tired, I will not quit.
Even though I was her in the past, I will become who I'm meant to be.

I use this mantra throughout the day to stay grounded, focused, and resilient.

It reminds me that even in the face of adversity, I will not falter.

Even though — I will.

Reflection Prompt:

Pause. Own the Excuses. Reclaim the Will.

Take a moment.
Breathe.
Now say them out loud: the reasons, the fears, the weight you're carrying.

Even though I'm exhausted.
Even though I've failed before.
Even though I don't feel strong enough.
Even though it would be easier to numb.
Even though I'm scared.
Even though the past still haunts me.

Now… Make your declaration.

I will get back up.
I will stay the course.
I will believe in who I'm becoming.
I will choose presence over escape.
I will keep going—even when it's hard.

Now write your own.
List every "Even though…"
And then follow it with your "I will."

Frenemies

Sobriety doesn't just change your habits. It changes your relationships.

You start seeing people for who they really are and who they were all along.

Some friendships were never rooted in truth. They were built on late-night chaos, half-remembered conversations, and a silent mutual agreement to stay numb together. It feels like loyalty, but it's just shared distraction. You kept them around because it was easier to laugh together than look underneath the hood.

And when you decide to break the cycle, to really change, some of those people don't know what to do with you.

They pull back.
They get uncomfortable.
They throw little jabs masked as jokes.
They miss the version of you that made their own life choices feel justified.

Because when you stop drinking, you don't just break up with the substance; you disrupt the system. And people who are still caught in it? They feel that disruption like a threat.

But that's not your burden to carry.

You're allowed to outgrow people who only knew how to love you when you were lost.
You're allowed to protect your peace, even if it means walking away from familiar faces.

Still, it's not all a loss.
Some friends will stay.
They will adapt. They'll ask questions. They support you without needing the old version of you to resurface.
They don't need you to be the life of the party to enjoy your presence.
They're not in it for the entertainment. They're in it for *you*.

Those friendships might shift, but they also deepen.
And they'll remind you: sobriety doesn't need to isolate you. It just filters the crowd.
What's left is real.

So don't cling to people just because you share a history.
Cling to the ones who can hold space for your future.
Let the rest slip through the cracks. That's where they belong.

You're not being harsh. You're being honest.

Because this new version of you doesn't want fake, she requires authenticity.

Reflection Prompt:

When you stopped drinking, who really showed up for *you*?

Which friendships feel strained now that you're no longer the same version of yourself?

Are you holding onto people out of loyalty, or because you're afraid of being alone?

Have you confused shared history with true connection?

What would it feel like to release relationships that no longer support your healing?

Not everyone is meant to go where you're headed.
So be honest:
Who are you still dragging along that's quietly holding you back?

Emotional Support Whiskey

There was always a glass on the nightstand.
A quiet companion.
A snifter of whiskey, waiting; just in case.
Just in case I couldn't sleep.
Just in case the silence got too loud.
Just in case my heart started racing for no reason at all.

It wasn't about getting drunk.
It was about knowing I *could*.
That if things got too heavy, I had a way out.
It felt like control. Like comfort. Like safety.
But it was none of those things.

It was dependency dressed up as ritual.
A coping mechanism I romanticized.
A lie I poured myself every night.

The truth?
It never gave me rest.
It never soothed me for long.
It numbed, yes—but numbing isn't healing.
It's a pause button on pain that keeps playing the same loop.

And I kept pressing it.

Trading clarity for fog.
Trading peace for a chemically-induced pause.
Trading healing for the illusion of "I'm okay."

What kind of self-love is that?

The kind that settles.
The kind that survives, not thrives.

But not anymore.

I've outgrown the need for "just in case."
Because now, I trust myself to sit with the storm.
To feel what's real.
To find peace in breath, not bourbon.

Healing isn't always loud. Sometimes it's quiet.
A nightstand with nothing on it.
A promise kept.
A woman choosing herself, over and over again.

Reflection Prompt:

What's your version of "just in case"?
That one thing you kept nearby to take the edge off, to feel in control, to survive the night.
Have you mistaken comfort for dependency?
What rituals have you romanticized that were actually holding you back?
What emotions were you trying to outrun or mute?
What truth were you afraid might surface in the silence?

Now consider:

What does true comfort look like, without the chemical escape?
What would it mean to rewrite that ritual into one of real self-love, not survival?

Deliberate Discomfort

Every Monday starts with a cold plunge.
Not for fun. Not for show.
But because it sets the tone: body, mind, and mission.

I choose discomfort. On purpose.
Because if I can sit in freezing water and stay calm,
Then I can walk into the week knowing I can do hard things.

That cold hits like a thousand needles.
Your body yells GET OUT. Your mind begs WHY are we doing this?!

And that's the exact moment I lean in.

To remind myself:
I run this.
I'm in charge.

Not fear.
Not doubt.
Not the excuses.

This is how I train my nervous system.
Push it into chaos, then breathe it back to balance.

Discipline isn't forged in comfort.
It's carved out in the places we resist and avoid.

Deliberate discomfort. Nervous system mastery. No more waiting for
the right mood—just action.
Let's f*cking go.

Reflection Prompt:

Do you believe you can do hard things?
When have you *proven* it to yourself?

Think back to a time you leaned into discomfort, whether physical, emotional, or mental.
What did it teach you about your strength, your limits, or your excuses?

How can you train your nervous system—not to avoid discomfort—but to breathe through it and rise?

What deliberate challenge can you take on this week to remind yourself:
You run this.
Not fear. Not doubt. Not the mood.
Just you, choosing to overcome.

Don't Be Messy

The last day I drank,
I said,
"I just wish killing myself wouldn't be so messy."
As if the cleanup would be the worst part.
As if my absence would only matter because of the inconvenience it
caused.

Even in my darkest moment,
I was still trying to make my suffering neat,
palatable for everyone else.
I didn't want to leave behind one more burden,
one more broken thing for someone to fix.
I just wanted to disappear…
quietly.
Cleanly.

Because for so long,
I believed I was the mess.
Too chaotic to love,
too loud to keep,
too much to carry.

The shame was suffocating.
It wrapped around me like a blanket I never asked for.
And the self-hate?
It was hidden.
Private.
A secret pain only I sat with, alone.

I was drowning
behind a composed face
and a heart quietly begging to be saved.

And then—
I finally said, "Enough."

Enough of the self-inflicted shame.
Enough of the pain, the regret, the poison I kept swallowing.
I prayed every night:
God, take this away from me. This urge, the craving, the need to drink.

And then, I surrendered.
And I rebuilt.

No more regret.
No more performing.
No more dying just to fit inside the box the world made for me.

I quit drinking.
I quit apologizing for my existence.
I quit putting other people's comfort above my own survival.

The mantra became: Strengthen. Build. Become.

Brick by brick,
With trembling hands and a defiant spirit,
I laid the foundation of my truth.
And there, in the ashes,
I met her—
The woman I had buried beneath the shame.

Not the mask.
Not the martyr.
Not the mess.

But the fighter.
The relentless.
The survivor.

I am no longer the mess.
I am the masterpiece.

Proof that resurrection is real.
That healing is holy.
That you can walk through your darkest night—
and still rise in the morning
radiant, grounded, and unapologetically alive.

Reflection Prompt:

Have you ever tried to make your pain more "palatable" for others? What parts of your suffering have you hidden, minimized, or made more acceptable so you wouldn't feel like a burden?

Who taught you that being messy made you unlovable?

What would it look like to *stop apologizing* for your existence? To take up space, not as a burden, but as a birthright?

The 3 Stages of Relapse

Let's get one thing straight: relapse doesn't happen the moment you pick up the drink. It happens in stages. It's a slow slide, not a sudden fall. And if you catch it early enough, you can stop the spiral before it turns into a damn tornado.

1. Emotional Relapse
You're not thinking about drinking—*yet*.
But your habits and headspace are starting to crack.
You're bottling things up, pulling away, skipping the things that keep you grounded. Maybe you're snapping more. Tired, anxious, restless. Your nervous system is screaming for regulation, and you're ignoring it.
What to do: Talk. Move. Sleep. Eat something real. Don't wait until you're in a full-blown spinout to check back in.

2. Mental Relapse
Here's where the tug-of-war begins.
Part of you wants to stay sober. The other part starts whispering: *"One drink wouldn't hurt."*
You start glamorizing the past, forgetting the hangovers and remembering the high. You bargain. You daydream. You start *planning*.
What to do: Play the tape all the way through. Not just the first drink, but the next day, the regret, the shame, the starting over. Reach out. Move your body. Refocus your mind. Re-anchor into your WHY.

3.   Physical Relapse

This is the part everyone sees: the actual drink.

But by this point? The other two stages have already worn you down.

You've convinced yourself it's fine. You've said F*ck it.

What to do: Get out of the situation. Call someone who gets it.

Remind yourself: this is bigger than tonight—it's your life.

Relapse isn't failure. It's feedback.

If it happens, don't drown in shame. Instead, study the data!

What did you miss? What were you feeling? What needs to shift?

Then get back up, and start again…wiser, not weaker.

You've got this. Stay awake. Stay honest. Stay in the fight.

Reflection Prompt:

Have you ever noticed the early signs before a relapse?

What were you feeling, avoiding, or telling yourself?

What does your *personal* warning system look like?

What thoughts or habits tend to creep in before things start to spiral?

Write about one tool, habit, or person that helps you pivot when you're headed down that road.

And if you've relapsed before, what did it teach you?

Not as a failure, but as *data*.

How can you use that insight to stay ahead of the cycle next time—and rewrite the ending?

And Then It Happened

Last night, we went out for my mom's birthday. The whole family was there, wine pouring, bourbon swirling (my old weakness), and drinks flowing long after we got home.

But here's the miracle:
I didn't want any of it.
Not a sip. Not even a second thought.
I felt calm. Grounded. Like me.

I've been praying every night for God to take the desire away, to make alcohol feel as toxic to me as drinking bleach.

And last night… it finally did.

That craving, the pull, the itch, it was gone.
In its place? Wholeness.

Not just the absence of alcohol.
But the presence of peace.
Like I'd come home to the version of me that existed before the bottle ever had a voice.

Reflection Prompt:

Have you ever experienced a moment where the craving was just…
gone?

Even if it hasn't happened yet, can you imagine what that would feel
like?
Not just resisting the urge, but *not having the urge at all.*

What would it mean to finally feel *free,* not because you fought the
drink, but because you didn't even want it?

Think about the version of you that exists without the pull of alcohol.

Go Play!

Sobriety isn't just about discipline; it's also about freedom.

Real fun.Real joy.
The kind that doesn't come with guilt or a hangover.

There's a wounded child inside you who didn't get enough light, enough laughter, enough room to just be.
That child still lives in you, and they're craving color, silliness, movement, play.

So today: dance, laugh, make a mess, be weird.
Healing happens here, too.

You're not just sober.
You're alive. You're Free, Go Play!

Reflection Prompt:

What part of you has been taking life a little too seriously lately?
Have you been so focused on healing that you've forgotten how to *live*?

What did joy look like before the world told you to grow up, toughen up, or calm down?
What's one small, playful act you can say yes to today that reminds your inner child they're safe, seen, and allowed to shine?

Observe, Don't Absorb.

As an empath, I've realized I used alcohol like armor, an invisible shield to block out the heavy energy I picked up from others.
At first, it felt like protection, but over time, I saw that it wasn't just blocking the outside world; it was also blocking my divine energy. My intuition, my discernment, and my true self.

I notice I'm most triggered when I absorb energy instead of observing it. Sobriety has been a journey of learning how to let energy pass through without letting it take root inside me.

I'm still working on finding healthier ways to cleanse and protect my energy.
I've also learned that many empaths tend to have a complicated, often toxic relationship with alcohol because of this dynamic.

Does this resonate with anyone else?

Reflection Prompt:

Do you know the difference between feeling your own emotions and absorbing someone else's?
What does it feel like in your body when you've taken on energy that isn't yours?
How did alcohol once help you cope, and how is sobriety teaching you to protect yourself differently?

Now that the "armor" is off, what are some healthy ways you can clear your energy, hold boundaries, and stay grounded in *your* truth?

Cortisol Face

At four weeks sober, I took a selfie and then looked back at an old one from when I was still drinking. I didn't expect to feel so called out by my own face. Swollen, tired, inflamed... that was *cortisol face* in full effect.

It's not just about puffiness. Alcohol floods your system with cortisol, the stress hormone, and when it stays high, it wreaks havoc on your body. For me, it wasn't just the face. My eyesight was off, and I couldn't go a day without glasses. My hair was thinning, my skin was dull, and I felt like I was falling apart slowly, from the outside in.

Some quick facts about alcohol and cortisol:

> It disrupts your sleep cycle, keeping cortisol elevated at night.
> High cortisol causes water retention and inflammation, especially in your face
> It weakens your immune system and slows healing
> It contributes to hair loss, skin issues, and premature aging

Honestly? Watching my face de-puff and my eyes light up again was a huge motivation. You don't need to be vain to care. It's a sign that your body is *finally* coming out of fight-or-flight and starting to feel safe again.

Take the picture. And then take your glow back!

Reflection Prompt:

What physical changes have you noticed before and after drinking?
Have you seen signs of stress in your face, skin, hair, or energy levels?

Be real with yourself:
Are there symptoms you've ignored or brushed off that might actually
be your body waving a red flag?

What would it mean to see your glow come back, not just for looks,
but as a reflection of healing, safety, and balance?

Take a moment to check in:
What is your body trying to tell you now that you're finally listening?

The Magician & The Alchemist

Years ago, during a yoga teacher training, we were asked to explore the wheel of archetypes and choose the one that resonated most.

I chose the Magician.

The shapeshifter. The chameleon. The master of deception.
All the things I had learned to be, out of necessity. I didn't know who I was, but I sure as hell knew how to become what everyone else needed. Or expected. Or would accept.
What I didn't realize back then was that I had bonded with the *shadow* side of the Magician.
The Illusionist.
The one who bends, hides, and manipulates perception, not out of malice, but survival.
The one who constantly scans the room, puts on the mask, and asks, *"Who do I need to be to entertain this crowd?"*

But there's another side to the Magician.
The light side.
The Alchemist.

The one who turns metal into gold. The one who transforms pain into purpose.

Carl Jung believed that alchemy wasn't really about turning metal into gold. He believed it was symbolic. It was about human transformation. It was the process of taking life's raw, messy material: Trauma, grief, failure, and turning it into something meaningful.

Recovery is alchemy.

It's doing the shadow work. It's looking at the parts of yourself you've kept buried, your flaws, your guilt, your patterns—and shining a big, bright fucking spotlight on them.

It's saying, *"Shapeshifting was the trick. But this transformation is the real magic."*

The Magician says, *"Hide this."*
The Alchemist says, *"Transmute it."*

And that's how you recover.
That's how you become whole.
That's how you make gold.

Reflection Prompt:

Which archetype has shaped your survival story?
Are you living from the shadow—performing, pleasing, pretending?
Or are you ready to do the work of the Alchemist—facing what you've hidden, owning your truth, and turning your pain into power?
What truth have you been disguising that's ready to be transformed?

Don't Get Hijacked

Whether you're on Day 1, just starting to contemplate change, or three years deep into recovery, **someone will try to hijack your journey**.

Sometimes it's subtle. A passive-aggressive comment.
A raised eyebrow. Other times it's a straight-up punch to the gut:
"Your opinion doesn't count until you've hit a year."
"AA is the only way."
"You're not really sober unless…"

Let me be clear: **Fuck that.**

People love to put limits on what they don't understand. They didn't see the nights you white-knuckled through the urge. They didn't hear the silent scream in your chest when you walked away instead of giving in. They don't know the *internal wars* you've already fought and won.

And even if they *did*, who are they to decide what matters?

You think one week sober isn't worth celebrating?

Do you think 24 hours of choosing yourself over destruction isn't a victory?

That mindset isn't recovery; it's ego in recovery clothes.

If you're here and doing this, you've already begun. You've already decided, even just slightly, that the old way isn't working. And that spark? That whisper of *maybe*? That's everything. That's how the fire starts.

So don't let anyone rob your comeback story.

Don't let their opinions hijack your motivation.

You are not here to meet someone else's approval.
You are here to rise.

And if life has taken its shots and you're still standing, still waking up and showing up, you're not behind.
You're **undefeated**.

You're breathing. You're alive. You're choosing better.
You're a fucking champion.

Reflection Prompt:

Has someone ever tried to hijack *your* recovery, or your progress, by minimizing it, questioning it, or trying to define it for you?

Whose voice are you listening to: yours, or someone else's?

You get to define what victory looks like.
So… what does *your* comeback story sound like?

The Tale of Two Wolves

There's an old story, often passed down from the elders, about a battle that rages within us all.

A grandfather tells his grandson:
"Inside every person, there are two wolves. **One is darkness:** *anger, addiction, shame, lies, and self-destruction.* **The other is light:** *truth, clarity, resilience, love, and healing. The two are always at war."*

The grandson thinks for a moment and then asks,
"Which one wins?"

The grandfather replies,
"The one you feed."

Sobriety is the daily decision to stop feeding the wolf that wants to watch your destruction, and to start nourishing the one that remembers who you were before the pain, before the numbing, before you forgot your own power.

Some days, that dark wolf still snarls. Still tempts. Still whispers old lies in a familiar voice.
But the longer you walk this path, the more you feed your strength, your truth, your clarity; the quieter that dark wolf gets.

This is the fight of your life.

So feed the right one.
Feed the one that's building you, not breaking you.
Because healing isn't about perfection, it's about choosing, again and again, to be better, to do better.
Even when it's hard.

Two wolves. One choice.
Every day. Every breath.
Feed the wolf that sets you free.

Reflection Prompt:

Which wolf have you been feeding lately?

Be honest, what thoughts, habits, or choices have you been nourishing?
Are they building you up… or breaking you down?

Now, reflect on this:
What does feeding your *light* wolf look like in your daily life, today, this week, this moment?

Great Adaptations

They said I had issues.
I had "symptoms." Labels. Diagnoses.
But no one ever told me that what looked like dysfunction…
It was actually devotion.
Every shutdown, every outburst, every time I reached for control or
a coping mechanism that hurt—
I wasn't being reckless.
I was trying to feel safe.

It took me years to understand that most of what I carried wasn't
"bad behavior."
It was my body doing whatever it took to survive.
To protect me.
To love me, in the only way it knew how.

Hypervigilance? That's not just anxiety—it's a nervous system
scanning for threat because it had to.
Dissociation? It's not failure to cope—it's the most intelligent way to
escape a body that felt like a battlefield.
Addiction? It's relief when your mind is too loud and your skin doesn't
feel like home.
People-pleasing, perfectionism, and silence? All survival strategies that say:
If I can just make everything okay out there, maybe I'll be okay in here.

You didn't choose trauma.
But your body chose *you.*

It fought for you.
It protected you.
It adapted for you.

And maybe those adaptations aren't serving you anymore.
Maybe they're now keeping you from the life, the love, the breath you deserve.

But instead of cutting those parts off in shame,
what if you turned toward them in gratitude?

Thank you for keeping me alive.
But I'm safe now. I can do it differently.

You're not broken.
You just bent.

Because surviving was never a weakness.
It was self-love in its fiercest form.

And now, healing is your next evolution.
Not by erasing who you've been…
But by becoming who you're ready to be.

Remember: Self-preservation is love in defense.
Healing is love in action.

Reflection Prompt:

When you think about the behaviors you feel ashamed of, can you trace them back to a moment of self-preservation?
What were you trying to avoid, escape, or survive? Can you honor the version of you that did what they had to do to make it through?

Now ask yourself:
What does self-love look like when it's no longer about defense, but about growth?
Where in your life can you start practicing love in action—not to protect yourself from pain, but to move toward peace?

Are You Coachable?

I don't just recognize trauma, I *understand* it. And I carried a relentless fire to help others claw their way out of the dark. That drive led me to become a certified psychedelic integration and transformational coach, working with veterans through incredible organizations that offered something rare and sacred: a chance to come home to themselves through psychedelic healing.

Day after day, I held space for warriors. I listened. I guided. I poured every tool, every insight, every ounce of myself into helping them break free, untangle their trauma, reclaim their power, and turn their pain into purpose. And I was *damn* good at it. Not because I was perfect, but because I *gave a shit*. I didn't want them to just survive; I wanted to see them *thrive*.

But here's what no one saw: behind the scenes, I was still barely holding on.

I was drinking to numb. Lashing out when I felt unseen. Drowning in anxiety and shame. Preaching healing while quietly unraveling in my own chaos.

And here's the truth that gutted me—I was asking them if they were doing the work, when I wasn't. Not really.

I had the knowledge. The credentials. The resources. I had everything… except the belief that *I* deserved to heal.

That's the part no certification prepares you for. You can't coach someone past the place you refuse to go yourself. And I had slammed headfirst into that wall.

So, I asked myself the same question I'd asked so many others: *Are you coachable?*

And for the first time, I answered honestly: No. Not yet.

Because until I believed *I* was worthy of being saved, I'd stay stuck in that hellish cycle; guiding others out of the fire while secretly burning alive.

Reflection Prompt:

You can read the books, listen to the podcasts, say all the right things… But are you actually *letting the work in*?

> Are you willing to hear hard truths without shutting down?
> Are you open to doing things differently, even if it feels awkward or uncomfortable?
> Are you ready to take real action, or just collect tools you'll never use?
> Do you *actually* want to change… or just want the pain to stop?

Being coachable means dropping the ego, the excuses, and the act. It means being honest with yourself first.

So be real:
Are you showing up to *transform*… or just to *look like* you are?

Ikebana – Expression Over Perfection

Ikebana is the Japanese art of flower arranging, but it's nothing like the Western version of stuffing a vase full of random flowers and calling it a day. It's meditative. Intentional. Minimal. And in early sobriety, it became a new hobby.

In the chaos of recovery—when I didn't know how to sit still or be in my body without a drink—Ikebana gave me something else to hold. Something that asked nothing of me except presence.

It taught me how to slow down without needing a reason.

In Ikebana, you don't force the flowers into place; you listen. You let each stem guide you. You don't fix or edit. You let the flower speak for itself.

That hit hard.
Because I'd spent years trying to fix and edit myself into something more acceptable. More appealing.

Ikebana mirrored everything recovery was trying to teach me:

> Minimalism — Cut the noise. Strip it back to what's real.
> Ma (space) — Make room. For silence. For discomfort. For breath.
> Natural form — Stop twisting yourself into what the world wants. Start honoring who you actually are.
> Impermanence — Nothing lasts. Not the chaos. Not the cravings. Not the shame. Like a flower that buds, blooms, and wilts—it's all temporary.

I didn't need to control.
I needed to be in relationship, with my emotions, my body, my mind.

Ikebana wasn't just flower arranging.
It was practicing the art of *expression and release.*
Of witnessing something rise and fall without interfering. Without forcing it. Without judgment. Just witnessing.

Sobriety isn't about holding it all together.
It's about learning how to *let go*: gracefully, deliberately, and with deep respect for whatever wants to come through in authentic expression.

Reflection Prompt:

Can you let something be imperfect and still see the beauty in it?
Where in your life do you need to release control and simply allow things to unfold?
What expressions have you been gripping too tightly? Can you let them rise, fall, and pass?

What hobby or creative outlet could help you practice presence, not perfection?
What's one healthy activity you're curious about that could support your healing?

The Language of Pain

I was scrolling TikTok the other day and saw a video:
Split screen.
On one side, the new chick fronting for Linkin Park.
On the other, Chester Bennington.

Same song.
Same lyrics.
But only one of them made my heart sink.

Chester wasn't performing; he was fucking purging.
I could feel the pain in his voice *bleeding out* like shrapnel cutting
straight through your soul.
It was lived in.
Heavy.
Real.

The new girl?
She was trying to sound angry. Trying to sound broken. It was forced rage.
But I could sense that she hadn't earned it.

And I said out loud:
"Oh shit. You can't fake pain."

Not real pain. Not the kind that splits you wide open and rearranges
who you are.

That kind of pain has a frequency.
It lives in your tone, your tongue, your gut.
You either speak it fluently, or you don't.

I tell my clients this all the time.
They come to me asking,
"I want to serve."
"I want to help people."
"I want to be a leader."

And I say...
Then learn to speak pain.
Because you can't lead anyone out of the dark if you've never sat in it.
You can't guide someone through their suffering with buzzwords and borrowed quotes.

You have to *know* it.
You have to carry it in your bones and speak it like it's your first language.
You have to stop running from it and start translating it.

And I will ask them:

What if all that trauma wasn't just damage?
What if it was your fluency test?
What if everything that broke you was teaching you how to speak the language of pain and the dialect of suffering?

Your trauma wasn't meant to destroy you.
It was meant to prepare you.
And the longer you avoid it, the longer you delay your purpose.

And that purpose?
It's forged in the struggle.
And people can hear the difference between someone who's *lived it*...
and someone who's forcing it.

So, no, you can't fake pain.

And if you've lived it?

Speak it.

Use it.

Let it mean something.

This was the moment everything shifted. I told myself, "Elaine, stop numbing. Face it head-on." It was time to untangle how my pain shaped my patterns, how my reactions became behaviors. To connect the dots and see that pain wasn't just a wound; it was a catalyst for my purpose. I had to understand it so I could finally speak it with clarity and truth.

Because the ones still suffering don't need a hero. **They need a translator.**

Reflection Prompt:

What if your greatest struggles weren't setbacks, but training grounds?

Look back on a painful chapter in your life.

What did it teach you about who you are, what you value, or what you're capable of?

If that pain was a teacher and not a punishment, what lesson was it trying to give you?

And how might that lesson be connected to your purpose?

Rebuild From the Inside Out

I'm learning that sobriety isn't just about not drinking, it's about rebuilding myself from the inside out. It's a total nervous system renovation, a mindset shift, a return to joy, and a reclaiming of peace. Here are the pillars that have been holding me up:

1.   Deliberate Discomfort
I've been leaning into the hard stuff on purpose.
Cold plunges, workouts, fasting, and even doing things I usually avoid or procrastinate on. Each time I choose discomfort, I'm teaching my brain: I can do hard things. I am in control. It's rewiring me from the inside out.

2.   Play & Joy
Yes, sobriety can be fun! I've been saying yes to life in small, unexpected ways—petting zoos, playing with my dogs, unique coffee shops, people-watching, planting/gardening, thrifting, exploring trails, cooking new meals, and soaking in sweet moments with my family. This is the joy I used to chase in a bottle—only now it's real, and I'm fully present for it.

3.   Metacognition & Mind Work
I've started noticing my thoughts instead of becoming them. Meditation, breathwork, and creative writing. These tools help me pause, reflect, and get curious instead of reactive. I'm not just surviving the day anymore, I'm observing it, shaping it, and showing up for it.

4.   Creating Peace

Peace isn't passive—it's something I create.

Reading, long walks, grounding barefoot in nature, hot baths, tidying up and decluttering my space, and most importantly, talking to myself with kindness. I used to be my own worst critic. Now I'm becoming my biggest ally.

None of this is perfect. Some days are still hard. But I'm stacking tools instead of regrets, and that feels damn good.

Reflection Prompt:

Which pillar resonates most with where you are right now?
Deliberate discomfort, play and joy, metacognition, or creating peace?
What's one small way you can strengthen that pillar this week?

Are you still trying to "white-knuckle" sobriety from the outside in, or are you ready to rebuild from the inside out?

And finally:
What's one new habit, hobby, or healing ritual you could add to your daily rhythm—not to escape your life, but to *enhance* it?

My Toolkit

Just wanted to share a couple of tools that have been helping me in early sobriety, especially when the brain fog, anxiety, and cravings hit hard.

Supplements:
I've been taking NAD+ and GABA, and they've made a noticeable difference.

- NAD+ supports cellular repair, energy, and brain function, which can take a hit after long-term alcohol use.
- GABA is a calming neurotransmitter that often gets depleted with alcohol, and supplementing it can help with anxiety, sleep, and emotional regulation.

Important note: Always consult your doctor or medical provider before adding new supplements, especially if you're on medications or have underlying health conditions.

Bonus Tool:
I've also been using ChatGPT as a built-in sober coach. It's surprisingly helpful and always available. You can ask it for:

Daily motivation or mantras.
Coping tools for cravings.
Nutrition and sleep tips.
Emotional support or even just a pep talk.
Podcast or Book recommendations.

I'll ask things like "What's a mantra for when I feel triggered?" or "Give me some healthy dopamine boosters today," and it helps to keep me grounded.

This path isn't easy, but it is doable.
Load your toolbox. Build your support. Keep showing up.

You've got this.

Reflection Prompt:

What's in your current recovery toolkit—and is it working for you? What tools help you feel calm, clear, and in control when things get hard?

Have you tried adding support for your *body* as well as your *mind*—like supplements, movement, or rest?

What's one new tool, habit, or practice you're curious about that could strengthen your foundation?

When the cravings or brain fog show up, what will you reach for—something that numbs, or something that heals?

Waiting for My Rock Bottom

I didn't have a big, dramatic ending.
No jail cell. No intervention. No waking up in a hospital bed—
… Oh wait, that *did* happen once.
And still, it wasn't enough.

Just a thousand little humiliations that should've been the final curtain call.
But I kept moving the goalpost.

"This isn't rock bottom," I told myself.
"I still have a house."
"I still have my kids."

"I still have my marriage."
"I still have a shred of respect left."

What the fuck was I waiting for?
To lose everything?
To be homeless, filthy, and eating out of a trash can behind a gas station?
For someone to look me in the eyes and say, *You're done*?

The truth is, I was terrified of quitting
because quitting meant facing myself.
Without the buffer.
Without the bullshit.

So, I kept drinking, hoping maybe the bottom would come and make the decision for me.

But rock bottom isn't a place.
It's a moment.
A reckoning.
A line in the sand.

And one day, I finally drew mine.
Not because I lost everything...
But because I realized I didn't need to.

I didn't need a full-blown rock bottom moment.
I just got sick and tired of standing on the edge, daring life to push me.

Reflection Prompt:

Rock bottom doesn't have to be dramatic to be real. Sometimes, the most powerful choice is walking away *before* you lose everything. You don't need a disaster to justify your decision to change—you just need to decide you're worth saving.

Are you waiting for everything to fall apart before you choose yourself? What "line in the sand" do you need to draw *now*, before life draws it for you?

Be Delusional

You want to do something big? Something bold? Something no one around you understands?

Good. Be delusional.

Be the kind of person who believes in things that don't exist *yet*. The kind of person who sees a possibility long before it shows up on a blueprint or a map. The first person to invent a computer? Delusional. The one who said we could trap lightning in a wire and call it electricity? Absolutely unhinged. The guy who looked at the moon and said, "I'm gonna walk on that"? Batshit crazy.

Until they did it.

People will laugh. They'll doubt. They'll roll their eyes, call it a waste of time, say, "Who the hell do you think you are?"
And your answer should be: **"F*ck you. Watch me."**

That's what it takes, a belief so stubborn, so ridiculous, so outrageously strong that people question your sanity. And not just the outside voices, but the one in your own head. You know the one— that bad wolf whispering: *You're not good enough. You're not ready. You're going to fail.*

Let that voice fuel you.
Prove it wrong.

You're not following a path, you're carving one. This is uncharted territory. You don't need permission, approval, or applause.
You need courage, vision, and a healthy dose of delusion.

Because that's where change happens.
That's where movements start.

And sobriety? That's one of the boldest, most delusional things you can do in a world that profits off your self-destruction.

So yeah, be delusional.
Be the kind of person who makes the impossible possible.

The world doesn't need more people playing it safe.
It needs more people willing to be called crazy and do it anyway.

Reflection Prompt:

What dream are you silencing because it sounds *too big*?

Are you waiting for permission to believe in yourself?

What would it look like to stop playing it safe—and start playing for keeps?

Whose doubt are you carrying like it's truth?
Can you let go of needing others to get it, and just *go get it*?

You don't need to be realistic.
You need to be relentless.

So… what's your "crazy" idea?
And are you brave enough to chase it like it's already real?

Gotta Earn My Gold Stars and Badges

High-functioning?
Can that even be a thing?

I gripped that title like it meant something, like it was proof I didn't
have a problem.
As long as I checked the boxes.
As long as the laundry was done, the house looked good, and I left in
nice clothes with a full face of makeup—
I was functioning, right?

And not just functioning—**winning.**
I wore that badge like it was some kind of achievement.
Each day, I crushed the checklist. Each time I pushed through the
hangover and still got it all done, I handed myself another gold star.
Another shiny badge to say, *"See? I'm fine."*

Like holding it all together while falling apart inside made me better
than the version of me who couldn't.

But no one saw the price I paid for those gold stars.
The mental gymnastics.
The rage cleaning.
The endless to-do list I had to dominate just to feel like I'd earned
the right to exist.

I treated productivity like penance.
Validation like currency.
And perfection? I had to wear it like a uniform.

And the days I couldn't keep up?
The days I couldn't earn my gold stars?
When I was too hungover, too sick, too empty to perform?
God, I hated myself.

I spit venom at my own reflection:
"You're disgusting."
"You're weak."
"Get your shit together."

But now?

Now that I've stopped drinking, I've stopped performing.
I've retired the badge. I threw away the star chart.
My house doesn't have to be perfect.
I don't have to be perfect.
I can rest. I can breathe. I can take a damn day off without feeling
like I've failed some invisible standard.

Because I'm not covering up chaos anymore.
I'm not hiding the wreckage behind curated photos and spotless counters.
I'm not blurring my pain with concealer and a badge that says "I
functioned today."

Recovery gave me that.
Not just the absence of alcohol, but the absence of the act.
The freedom to be whole, enough, a real human, not a high-
functioning lie.

Reflection Prompt:

We don't just chase gold stars—we start to build our entire identity around them. Productivity becomes proof. Perfection becomes survival. But recovery asks a different question: *Who are you when you stop performing?*

What roles, routines, or rewards have you used to prove your worth?
What did "high-functioning" really look like for you, and what did it cost?
Who are you beneath the makeup, the checklist, the spotless home?
Can you give yourself permission to rest without guilt?
What could the future look like if you didn't have to prove your worth daily?

Sometimes Progressive Ain't Progress

It always starts off fun, doesn't it?

A drink at the party. A glass of wine with dinner. Beers at the game. Cocktails at brunch. You're just being social, normal. You're a cool mom. You're not *that person*. You've got this under control.

Until you don't.

Then life throws a curveball: stress, heartbreak, a trauma you didn't see coming, and suddenly that "glass with dinner" turns into wine at lunch, a nightcap before bed, maybe just something to take the edge off. You're not just drinking anymore. You're numbing. Managing. Coping.

But slowly, stealthily, it creeps in.

The number of drinks goes up. The occasions get less important, and everything becomes a reason to drink. The hangovers get worse, but you've still got responsibilities, so you reach for the Bloody Mary or the mimosa. Morning booze that feels "socially acceptable," like somehow, champagne at 10 a.m. makes it all okay.

And then one day… you're not sipping for fun. You're shooting to survive.

One to take the edge off. One to chase away the anxiety. One to outrun the shame, the guilt, the crash. You're stuck in the loop—drink to feel better, drink because you feel worse. And every dopamine dump leaves you with more depression than the last.

You ask yourself: How the hell did I get here?

It was all fun and games, not that long ago.

You still don't feel like *"that person."* But you can't deny the truth: you're caught. You're stuck. And you're tired.

This is what they mean when they say alcohol is a progressive disorder. It doesn't show up like SEAL Team 6, to kick down the door. It shows up in yoga pants, with a wine glass that says "Mommy Juice." It starts as a release and ends as a requirement.

Here's what's going on: Alcohol messes with your brain chemistry. At first, it floods your system with dopamine, that feel-good chemical, the reward hit that says "Ahhh, that helps." But the more you drink, the more your brain adapts. It stops making as much dopamine on its own. It actually dysregulates the receptors that feel pleasure, so now you need more just to feel okay. And without it? You feel dull, anxious, and irritable.

Meanwhile, it's messing with your GABA and glutamate, the systems that help you stay calm, focused, and relaxed. Over time, your brain loses its ability to regulate stress naturally. That's why the anxiety comes crashing in, sleep goes to shit, and abstinence makes your nervous system start screaming for its bottle to soothe itself.

It's not just in your head. It's in your wiring.

And once it's got you, it doesn't want to let go.

But here's what alcohol doesn't tell you:

You can unlearn this.
You can heal your brain.
You can take your power back.

The same brain that adapted to drinking can adapt to living without it again.

It's not easy.
It's not instant.
But it is possible.

Reflection Prompt:

It doesn't happen all at once. Alcohol doesn't ruin your life in a single night—it sneaks in, rewires your brain, and convinces you that dependence is normal. What starts as a treat becomes a trap. But here's the truth: just as your brain adapted to the cycle, it can adapt to freedom. Healing begins the moment you stop romanticizing the "normal" and start questioning what it's costing you.

When did your drinking shift from enjoyment to escape?
What signs did you ignore because it still looked "normal" from the outside?
How has your brain and body been asking for help through anxiety, exhaustion, or mood swings?
What would it look like to start rewiring your brain one choice, one day at a time?

Psychedelic Healing

Psychedelics didn't save me
They didn't erase the wreckage or hand me a clean slate.
They didn't fix my relationships or silence the storms inside.

But they did something else.
They turned on the light.
They held up the mirror and whispered,
"Don't look away—look within."

They called the parts of me home—
The girl who once dreamed,
The woman who fought,
The mother who carried,
The wild one who remembered.

They didn't hand me freedom.
They pointed to the key I'd been holding all along.

The messages didn't just come in the ceremony.
They often came in the quiet.
The sauna, where my breath slowed and the truth rose.
The shower, where I'd press my hands to the wall and silently plead,
"Why can't I heal? What's wrong with me?"

And the medicine would answer—not loudly, but clearly:
"You already know."
"You've always known."

I denied that voice for years.
Buried it beneath noise, distraction, and fear.
But it waited.
In the stillness.
In the silence.

Psychedelics don't do the work for you.
They show you what work *must* be done.
And once you see it—once you *know*—
You can't un-know.

This path is yours now.
Walk it.
Crawl it if you must.
But don't pretend you don't hear the truth in the silence.

Reflection Prompt:

Have you ever felt a whisper inside? Something deeper than thought—nudging you to look within?

What truth have you been avoiding, not because you don't know it, but because it asks you to change?

Can you recall a moment in the stillness: a shower, a walk, a breath, when you felt something in you, *remember*, who you really are?

What part of yourself is asking to come home now?

And most importantly:
Now that you've heard that quiet voice, even for a moment… will you finally honor it, or keep turning away?

Don't Run, Integrate.

Reinventing yourself doesn't mean running from your past; it means owning it and overcoming shame from past mistakes.

You don't change by abandoning who you used to be. You change by facing it head-on. Every version of you: the wild one, the hurting one, the one who just didn't know any better—they weren't mistakes. They were foundations. They carried your story. They kept you going. And they sparked the fire that brought you here.

True growth doesn't come from erasing your past; it comes from integrating it. From turning pain into wisdom. From learning to hold compassion for the parts of you that were just trying to survive. That didn't know any other way.

Yes, people can change. But it takes truth. Accountability. And the courage to walk through the fire instead of around it.

And when you earn that transformation? No one can take it from you.

Reflection Prompt:

Is there a version of you you're still ashamed of, or trying to forget? What would happen if, instead of running from that version, you sat with them, listened, and thanked them for surviving?

What pain are you ready to turn into wisdom? What would it look like to fully own your story—not just the polished parts, but the raw, messy chapters too?

Are you willing to stop running and start integrating?

Diagnosing the Human Condition

Have you ever watched one of those commercials?

"Are you tired? Feeling down? Irritable? Trouble sleeping? Trouble focusing?"

And you're sitting there like… yeah, that's called being a human.

But instead of telling you that's normal, they tell you it's a problem. A disorder. A chemical imbalance. And don't worry; they've got a pill just for that.

This is how we got here.

This is how we trained an entire society to believe that normal human emotions are symptoms that need to be fixed.

Sadness? Medicate it.

Anger? Suppress it.

Restlessness? Sedate it.

Discomfort? Escape it.

No wonder we're in a mental health and addiction crisis.

We've stopped teaching people how to feel and started teaching them how to numb.

We've convinced people that being fully alive is a disorder.

But here's the truth:

It is normal to feel down some days.

It is human to be overwhelmed, annoyed, restless, or heartbroken.

You're not broken, you're a fucking Human Being.

You don't need to shovel pills down your throat to dismiss the parts of you that feel.

You don't need to fix emotions that were never problems to begin with.

Because the real sickness?

Is a world that tells you your emotions were a diagnosis.

That told you your pain made you defective.

That sold you silence instead of support.

But you're not too much.

You're not unwell for having feelings.

You're alive.

In this recovery, we get to work on the root cause and stop putting Band-Aids over bullet holes.

This time, we get to raise a big middle finger to the society that profits off our disconnection and decide that feeling it all might just be the most rebellious act of healing a human can do.

Disclaimer:

This entry is not dismissing real mental health conditions or the value of professional treatment for diagnosable disorders. Therapy, medication, and clinical support save lives, and for many people, they are essential and life-changing tools.

What I'm talking about here is the cultural tendency to *symptomize normal human emotions*—to treat everyday experiences like sadness, fatigue, anxiety, or irritability as problems that must be medicated rather than understood.

This is about reclaiming our right to feel without immediately pathologizing our emotions. It's about making space for discomfort, not denying the importance of mental health care.

Reflection Prompt:

Somewhere along the way, we were taught that feeling sad meant we were depressed, feeling tired meant we were dysfunctional, and feeling angry meant we needed to calm down or be medicated. But emotions aren't diagnoses, they're data. They're signals. They're part of being fully, wildly human. The goal isn't to *fix* your feelings—it's to *feel* them and learn from them.

What emotions have you been taught to see as "bad" or "broken"?
How have you tried to mute or escape feelings that were actually trying to guide you?
What would it look like to let yourself feel without judgment?
Can you start honoring your emotions as messengers, not symptoms?

If You Love It, Set It Free

A friend of mine, an ex-Navy SEAL turned well-known podcaster, once said something to me that's echoed for twenty years. I was deep in heartbreak, clinging to a relationship I felt slipping away. He looked at me and said:

"If you love him, set him free. If he doesn't come back, he was never yours to begin with."

I wasn't ready to hear it back then. But the wisdom has unfolded over time.

Sobriety taught me the same lesson. I thought alcohol was part of me—something I couldn't live without. But when I finally let it go, I realized:
I don't want it back.
Because it was never love.
It was a habit.
It was an
escape.
It was an
illusion.

We grip so tightly to what we fear losing: relationships, substances, control, old identities. But clinging doesn't hold things close. It just keeps us stuck.

If it's real, it stays.
If it's meant, it grows.
If it's yours, it returns.
And if it doesn't?
You've freed yourself from something that was never meant to be.

Letting go isn't weakness.
It's strength.
It's self-trust.
It's knowing what's meant for you won't need to be held by force.

In sobriety.
In love.
In parenting.
In life.

(And BTW, that guy I set free came back and he's still mine!)

Reflection Prompt:

Letting go doesn't mean you didn't care.
It means you've stopped trying to force what was never meant to stay.

What are you afraid will happen if you let go?

Is this love, or just a fear of being without?

Have you mistaken attachment for connection?

What would it look like to release this with grace, instead of guilt?

Not everything we lose is a loss.
Sometimes it's the beginning of finally coming home to yourself.
So... what are you ready to set free?

Gracefully Bow Out

I want to be careful with this, because I know AA has helped a lot of people.
But for me? It wasn't healing. It was triggering.

I walked in hoping for support and direction.
What I got was noise.

Too many opinions. Too many people telling me what I should do, how I should feel, who I should be.
It felt like a room full of people projecting their story onto mine.
And in the process, I lost my voice.

I heard things like:
"Taking psychedelics to help your mental health is the dumbest thing I've ever heard."
"You're too smart to be sober. You have to be dumber to surrender."

That one still stings.
Like being told intelligence and recovery can't co-exist.

But the hardest part?
It awakened the very thing I was trying to heal:
The people-pleaser. The chameleon. The girl who shaped herself to be accepted.

I found myself saying what I thought they wanted to hear.
Nodding along when I disagreed.
Dimming myself just to belong.

That wasn't healing.
That was just another place where I abandoned myself to make others feel comfortable.

From my experience, AA felt rigid, shame-based, and dogmatic—run by well-meaning volunteers, sure, but lacking any formal training in harm reduction or evidence-based recovery.

AA wasn't necessarily the villain. But it wasn't my room.
I only wish more people within AA understood that recovery isn't linear.
It's not one-size-fits-all.
And insisting that it is? That harms other people's recovery.

Want to know the most important lessons I learned while I was there?

Sometimes, the bravest thing you can do for your healing...
is to walk out of a room that makes you smaller.

Reflection Prompt:

Have you ever stayed in a space that felt misaligned just because you didn't want to disappoint others?
What signs did your body or intuition give you that it wasn't right for you?

Where in your life are you still dimming your light to fit in or feel accepted?

What different modalities have helped you the most along the way?

And finally:
Can you trust that walking away from what's not meant for you *is* an act of healing, not failure?

Why Don't You Just Meet Me in the Middle

Alcohol gives you the highest highs and the lowest lows. I read somewhere that *"alcohol doesn't create more dopamine—it just steals it from tomorrow."* And isn't that the truth?

When I first got sober, that terrified me. I didn't just grieve the substance—I grieved the version of myself I was when I was drinking. Would I ever feel that wild euphoria again? Would music still move me enough to dance and scream the lyrics like no one was watching? Would I still have those deep, tear-filled conversations at 2 a.m.? Would I ever laugh until I cried doing the kind of dumb, impulsive shit that only alcohol seemed to give me permission for?

I started thinking about all this last night, at my first sober concert.

Was it fun?
Yes.
Was it over-the-top, chaotic, mind-blowing fun?
No.

But it was the *right* amount of fun. I didn't borrow joy from tomorrow. I didn't wake up in a fog, questioning what I said or did. No shame. No regret. Just clarity. Pride. Peace.

That was the real high. The one that came the next morning. And it made the more tempered version of fun the night before feel worth it. Because this life? It's no longer a rollercoaster. It's steadier. More manageable. More honest.

Do I still miss the high sometimes? Of course.
But I don't miss the crash.

And that's the trade-off.
Maybe I'm not chasing the extremes anymore.
Maybe now, I'm just learning to meet myself in the middle.

Reflection Prompt:

Are you still chasing the all-or-nothing version of life to feel like it matters?
What quiet, unexpected joys have shown up since you stopped trying to live at full tilt?

Can you release the chaos without losing your sense of wonder?

What does it look like to meet yourself with honesty, balance, and ease today?
And could it be that the peace you've been craving isn't found in the high or the low…

But right here,
In the middle?

The Trifecta:
Anxiety, Depression, Panic

The first time I tried to quit, I didn't make it far.

Anxiety had me by the throat: tight chest, racing thoughts, always bracing for the worst. Panic attacks came out of nowhere. One minute I was in the grocery aisle, the next I was ditching my cart and speed-walking to the parking lot, trying not to flip out.

And when anxiety finally stepped aside, depression rolled in like a thick fog. Everything felt heavy. Nothing mattered. I wasn't living, I was enduring.

Then came the voice:
"You know what would fix this…"
And just like that, I was drinking again.

I used to say I "just wasn't ready yet."
But the truth?
I still believed alcohol helped. I thought it was my medicine.
I clung to it like a lifeline—even when I knew it was slowly killing me.

That first attempt felt like punishment. Like something was being taken from me.
Like someone had snatched away my favorite toy, and I was throwing a full-blown tantrum, screaming, *"I want it back!"*

That's how tightly I held onto the thing that was breaking me.

This time? Different.

The first three weeks were still brutal, no detox, no rehab, just me and the war in my head.

But I stayed. I showed up. I didn't run.

And slowly, the grip loosened.

Panic faded.
Anxiety and depression backed off.
They still visit from time to time, but they don't own me anymore.
I know how to handle those little bastards.

And here's the truth:

The trifecta isn't a weakness. It's an alarm system.
It's your body screaming, *"This isn't who you are."*
It's cognitive dissonance in action. When your behavior doesn't match your truth, and your nervous system starts crashing out.

Alcohol didn't soothe the trifecta.
It created it.

That first time around, I thought sobriety stole something from me.
Like someone took my toy and stuck me in a time-out.
Poor me. No fun. No buzz. No escape.

But this time? I see it clearly.

Sobriety isn't a punishment.
It's an offering.
It started giving me everything I *thought* alcohol would: peace, clarity, freedom.

And that's the difference this time around:

Sobriety doesn't take.
It gives.

Reflection Prompt:

Have you ever mistaken a coping mechanism for medicine?
What "lifelines" are you still clinging to, even if they're slowly breaking you?
Can you recognize anxiety, depression, and panic not as flaws, but as signals that something needs to change?
What if the thing you fear giving up is the thing holding you back from becoming who you truly are?

"I Am"

Years ago, a therapist looked me in the eyes and asked, "Who are you? Who is Elaine Brewer?"
So, naturally, I started listing off: Mom, Wife, Daughter, Sister, Homemaker…
She stopped me and said, "No, those are your roles. *Who are you?*"

Holy shit. I was speechless.
I didn't know what to say.
I couldn't think of a single thing that described me without being attached to a role.

It wasn't until years later—after a plant medicine retreat—that it finally clicked. I had my answer.
So here is my "I Am" statement:

I am a caregiver. A fierce supporter. A protector of the vulnerable and a safe place for the misunderstood.

I am a nurturer to those who need care, a voice for those who struggle to speak, and a warrior for those who cannot fight for themselves.

I am a partner. A loyal companion, a steady anchor, a keeper of heart and home. I give love fully, hold space deeply, and show up with strength and softness in equal measure.

I am relentless to the core. A listening ear, a grounding presence, and when needed, a force to be reckoned with.

I am a Patriot. A truth seeker. I stand rooted in freedom and country, shaped by experience, and led by principle, not party.

I am a believer. A Christian, a mystic, a student of the universe. I walk with Spirit, guided by faith, energy, and divine curiosity. I hold reverence for magic, mystery, and the sacred in all things.

I am nature. I am the wolf spirit. A feral and wild woman. A healer with plants, a whisperer of animals, a seeker of the earth's wisdom.

I am energy. I carry the sun and the moon within me. I am both masculine and feminine, both quiet and bold. I live in the rhythm of connection and the pulse of life.

I read the Bible and the Sutras. I pray and I meditate. I burn sage and charge crystals. I wear the cross and fly the flag.

I am an anomaly. I am many things. I do not conform. I will not be boxed, diminished, or silenced.

Do not be confused or intimidated by me, but stand in awe of my uniqueness.
There is only one me.

I am Elaine Brewer.

Reflection Prompt:

If everything was stripped away: your job, your home, your partner,
Your children—*who are you? What is the essence of You?*
What qualities would remain that no one can take from you?
And if you can't name them yet...
Who do you want to be?
Write that.
And start becoming her.

I'll Never Drink Again

When you finally say, *I'll never drink again*—and believe it—it's not just a decision. It's the result of relentless effort, deep change, and a soul-level remembering of who you are.

You've made it through the hard nights.
You've tasted peace you created yourself.
You've woken up without shame, without a hangover, and with pride.

This moment? It's not for beating yourself up over the past.
It's for standing tall in the now.

Reflect on how far you've come.
Celebrate your grit.
Honor your strength.

And above all, remember your *why*, carry it like a battle flag into whatever comes next.
Because raw-dogging life? It's one of the hardest things a person can do.

If it were easy, everyone would do it.
They don't.
But you are.

Reflection Prompt:

When you said, *"I'll never drink again,"* what did that moment hold for you?
Has it happened yet, or are you still searching for the conviction to say it and mean it?

What has it taken to get this far?
What do you still need to believe, feel, heal, or fully commit to?

Now ask yourself: what anchors you?
What keeps you grounded when the urge to escape whispers in?

If that urge ever returns, what kind of support—internal or external—will help you stand firm?

And today, in this moment, what does *freedom* feel like in your body, your mind, and your life?

Lay Her to Rest

In sobriety and trauma recovery in general, I often see people get stuck in the loop of trying to rewrite their wrongs. Don't get me wrong: accountability matters. Real apologies, making amends, and creating lasting change are non-negotiable. But when you start obsessing over the past, constantly trying to fix what can't be undone, you end up trapped. Frozen. Unable to grow.

The truth is, the people you've hurt will either forgive you or they won't. They'll either believe in your ability to change or they'll stay rooted in who you were. You can't control that.

What you *can* control is who you become next. The most powerful apology you'll ever give is your evolution. You don't prove remorse by staying stuck in shame—you prove it by becoming someone who no longer resembles the person who caused harm.

Say the apologies. Make the amends. Then lay that past version of yourself to rest.

You're not her anymore. You're new. You're growing. Now prove it.

Reflection Prompt:

How long do you plan to carry the weight of a woman you no longer are?

Are you holding onto shame because you think it makes you accountable?

Is your healing about becoming whole, or just trying to make others believe you've changed?

What would it look like to forgive the version of you who didn't know better?

Can you honor your past without letting it define your future?

You don't owe the world a performance of regret.
You owe yourself a chance to be free.
So, ask yourself:
Is it time to lay her to rest, and finally become who you're meant to be?

The Courage to Be Seen

The bravest thing you can do is choose to be seen: raw, authentic, and vulnerable.

God didn't load me up with fancy talents or polished skills. But *He* gave me three things: the ability to feel deeply, the gift of words, and one hell of a story.

For years, I battled my demons in silence. Hiding the mess. Smiling through the pain. Carrying the weight alone because I thought I had to.

But not anymore.

I've found the courage to be seen, not just the highlight reel, but the truth. The cracks. The healing. The whole damn thing.

I hope that by telling my story, someone else will find the strength to tell theirs. That my voice might unlock yours. That you'll stop hiding and start healing. That you'll remember you're not alone in the dark, and you don't have to stay there.

So here I am.
No more masks.
No more hiding.
Now you see me.

Reflection Prompt

What parts of you are still hiding in the dark or masking?

Are you showing the world your truth, or just the parts you think are acceptable?

What would it look like to stop performing and start *revealing*?

Can you believe that your honesty might be the exact thing someone else needs to hear?

Act As If

There's a scene in the movie *Boiler Room* where Ben Affleck's character walks into a room full of hungry Wall Street recruits and delivers a line I've played on repeat more times than I'd like to admit:

"Act as if. You understand what that means? Act as if you are the fucking president of this firm. Act as if you've got a nine-inch c*ck. Okay? Act. As. If."

Arrogant? Yep.
Crude? Absolutely.
Motivating as hell? Without a doubt.

That phrase has carried me through interviews, speeches, training workshops—any moment where fear crept in and imposter syndrome whispered, *You don't belong here.* That's when I'd shift gears and *Act As If.*

Act as if you've done it a hundred times.
Act as if you were born to lead.
Act as if failure isn't even on the table.

And here's the thing: it works.

In recovery, this growth mindset is essential. You have to *embody* the version of you that you're fighting to become, long before it feels natural. In week one, when someone offers you a drink, and you say *"I don't drink"* instead of *"I'm taking a break,"* That's identity-level rewiring. That's a power move.

Because the words you choose aren't just words, they're declarations.

And that's why I'll never understand people five years into sobriety still saying, *"I'm an alcoholic."* That's a *fixed mindset.* That's anchoring yourself to the very identity you worked so hard to escape.

Try this instead:
"I've healed from substance abuse."
"I broke up with alcohol."
"I quit."
"Nah, I'm good—I don't need it."

You remember those "I Am"statements? What you say about yourself matters. Manifesting isn't some mystical force—it's repetition, energy, and choosing your future with intention. So, when you say *"I'm an addict, I'm powerless, I'll always struggle"*—ask yourself, is that the *truth*, or is that *a self-defeating belief?*

If that model works for you, great. But don't bring that energy over here. I'm working with a growth mindset.

So even if you're scared... even if you feel like a fraud...

Walk in like you own the place.
Speak like you're the expert.

Act as if...

Until *You Are.*

Reflection Prompt:

Are you living it, or just saying it?

> Do your habits reflect the person you're becoming—or the one you're trying to leave behind?
> Are you waiting to *feel* confident, or are you choosing to *act* like someone who already is?
> When the pressure's on, do you fall back into the old story—or stand in the new one you're writing?
> What would it look like to stop just *talking* recovery and start *walking* it?
> So… are you acting like the old you?
> Or the one you swore you'd become?

T.O.M.S.

I used to have it bad.

T.O.M.S: Terrified of Missing Shit.
If there was a party, I was there. A concert? Count me in. Random invite from someone I barely knew? Let's go. I didn't want to miss the moment, the memory, the story. I wanted to feel alive, connected, part of something. But if I'm being honest… it wasn't about the people or the experience. It was about opportunity, it was about the alcohol, always.

I said yes because it gave me a reason to drink.

Now that the drinking's gone, so is the urgency. That fear of missing out? It's evaporated. I scroll through social media and see the same highlight reels; vacations, champagne toasts, curated friend groups with mile-wide smiles and I feel… nothing.

Because I've learned something:
The people who try the hardest to look happy are often the ones trying to convince themselves they are.

These days, I crave stillness more than stimulation. My house is my safe place. My family is my Tribe. The idea of going out sounds nice in theory but the reality rarely lives up to the hype. Most of the time, I come home feeling overstimulated, underwhelmed, and more committed than ever to protecting my peace.

T.O.M.S. used to run my life.
Now?

I'm not afraid of missing shit out there—
I'm afraid of missing what's right here.

And that's the shift that changed everything.

Reflection Prompt:

Has your definition of "fun" changed?
What used to excite you that now just feels exhausting?

Think about the last time you went out because you felt like you
should—not because you actually wanted to.
What were you hoping to find out there?
What did you actually come home with?

Now ask yourself:
What are you truly afraid of missing—*the moment… or the distraction?*

And what might you *gain* by staying in, being present, and honoring
your peace instead?

Creating Safety in a Mind that Hates You

It's hard to feel safe in a mind that feels like it's turned against you. That's why the escape becomes so addictive. When your own thoughts feel like the enemy, substances start looking like salvation.

You get that temporary relief, the kind that makes you feel confident, talkative, alive. Like maybe *this* version of you is the real you. But the high never holds. The crash is brutal. And when the mask slips, what's underneath feels unbearable: shame, disgust, regret. So, you run right back to the thing that lets you disappear.

It becomes a battle between your **True Self** and the version you've been surviving as—**Ego**. One side whispers: *Stay here. Feel this. Let's heal.* The other screams: *Retreat. Escape. Pretend everything's fine.*

And if you've been in fight-or-flight long enough or started numbing before you ever even knew who you were, then of course the ego wins. It's the devil you know. The version of you that knows how to perform, deflect, and numb the ache.

That's why the pause matters. Why abstinence matters, even if only temporarily. Not because it makes you "good" or "clean," but because it gives you space to *remember*. To reintroduce yourself to the True Self. To sit with them long enough to *see* them. Maybe even trust them again.

That version of you might not be polished, loud, or certain. But they're *real*. They want healing. They want peace. And they won't sell you out for a quick fix.

The ego helped you survive, but healing demands truth. And truth doesn't live in the performance. It lives in the version of you that's done pretending. It lives in the Higher Self. And it's time to get reacquainted.

Reflective Prompt:

Think about the voice in your head, the one that pushes you to perform, to stay busy, to numb out, to keep it all together. That's the ego. It's not evil, it's just scared. It's the part of you that learned how to survive, not how to heal.

Now think about the other voice, the quieter one. The one who wants peace. That asks you to slow down. That reminds you there's more to life than just getting through it. That's your Higher Self.

Can you tell the difference?

Sometimes it helps to give your ego a name. That way, when it shows up, you can recognize it, speak to it, and remind it who's in charge.

Naming the ego allows your True Self to step into the conversation with compassion, not judgment. It's not about silencing the ego—it's about learning how to lead it instead of letting it lead you.

Write down the ways your ego shows up. What does it sound like? What does it tell you? How does it try to protect you?

Now write from the voice of your Higher Self. What would they say back? What would they want you to know? What would it feel like to trust Self more than Ego?

The Hero's Journey

It didn't start with clarity.
It started with a pause.

100 days. No alcohol.
No numbing. No noise. Nowhere to hide.

Just me—face to face with the story I'd spent years spinning.

And what surfaced?

A loop of lies I'd mistaken for identity:
"I'm not safe."
"I don't belong."
"I feel too much."

"I'm Unlovable."
"Life keeps happening to me."
"Maybe I'm not cut out for this world."

That story? I didn't just inherit it, I kept choosing it.
And alcohol? It was the co-author.
Sure, it dulled the pain. But it kept the script alive.

This is how the story would unfold:

Wake up believing you're a piece of shit.
Drink to quiet the voice.
Drink too much.

Do something a piece of shit would do.
Wake up ashamed.
Repeat.

A fucking self-fulfilling prophecy.

But when I finally cut the cord,
no drinks, no distractions.
I met the unfiltered, unedited version of me.

And it hit me:

I wasn't a victim.
I was the one holding the pen.

Joseph Campbell called it The Hero's Journey. **The Hero's Journey** is a classic story pattern where the hero leaves their ordinary world, faces challenges that change them, and returns transformed. It's not just a myth—it's a map for personal growth. We all have moments when we're called to step away from what we know, face what scares us, and come back stronger.
But here's the part no one tells you,
To cross the threshold into the unknown,
you have to finally get sick of your old bullshit story.

And I did.

That 100-day pause?
That was my threshold.

Two choices:
Keep playing the victim,
or start writing the script where I save myself.

There was no rescue mission.
No white knight.
Just me, deciding to torch the old narrative
and write something new.

Now the page reads:
Wake up grateful.
Own the day.
Find the blessings.
Stay present.
Go to bed proud.
Repeat.

You either stay the damsel in distress
or you mount the hell up and become the fucking hero.

Recovered. Clear. Relentless

This isn't a fairy tale.
It's life: raw, brutal, beautiful, and unwritten.

This is where you *earn* your ending,
one honest and intentional day at a time.

You're the author now.
So, ask yourself:

What's it gonna be?
Who does your character become?

Reflection Prompt:

Sometimes it takes 100 days of silence, sobriety, and stripped-down truth to finally hear the story you've been telling yourself all along. That pause? It's not the end, it's the threshold. The moment you step out of the old script and into the unknown. The real adventure isn't out there, it's in *You*, and finally becoming who you were always meant to be.

What stories have you been telling yourself about who you are and what you're capable of?
Where have you been waiting for a rescue instead of writing your ending?
What's the old script you're finally ready to burn?
What does your new chapter sound like, and what needs to happen to become the hero of your own story?

Checkmate

Sobriety isn't some soft choice—it's a Power Move.
It's standing in a world that glamorizes the escape and choosing to stay present, sharp, and unwavering.

You're not sipping your way through life; you're grabbing it by the balls and declaring:
I don't need a drink to handle my shit. I run this. I am the master of my universe.

You feel your emotions instead of drowning them.
You face your past instead of hiding from it.
You create your own joy, your own peace, your own fun, without poisoning yourself to get there.

It's not lame.
It's not missing out.
It's f*cking legendary.

You're breaking the rules.
You're shattering the narrative that says you need alcohol to be social, sexy, relaxed, and alive.
And in doing so, you're proving something dangerous, something powerful:

You don't need anything to be enough. **You already are.**

This is what real confidence looks like.
Not loud and reckless, but steady, controlled, and untouchable.

This isn't restriction.
This is rebellion.

This isn't limitation.
This is freedom.

Yes, it's hard.
Yes, it takes time, strength and grit.
But that's because you're getting dialed the f*ck in. You are moving and thinking with intention and purpose. This time you get to say, Checkmate.

Reflection Prompt:

What would it look like to stop playing defense and make your move?

> Are you still trying to *cope*… or are you ready to *conquer*?
> What lies have you been sold about what alcohol adds to your life?
> Can you sit in your power without needing something to take the edge off?
> Where are you still underestimating just how strong, clear, and unstoppable you are?

This isn't weakness.
This is a strategy.
This is the moment you stop reacting and start *leading the game*.

So… what's your next power move?

I'm Sorry.

I don't even know who I'm apologizing to exactly—maybe to everyone. My friends, my family, my loved ones. But most of all, I'm sorry to myself. For thinking I was the exception to the rule.

It was never about hiding things to be deceitful or distant—I just didn't know how to share the weight of it.

I had been living a lie for so long, running on autopilot with "I'm fine," that I almost believed it myself.

Until I wasn't.

But by then, the story was so rehearsed, so deeply embedded, that I didn't know how to unravel it without everything else coming undone, too.

I told myself people would judge me. That I'd ruin my career. That I'd be seen differently, and I clung on to my deepest fear. Being a burden.
I didn't want to put my shit on someone else's plate.

And the irony? This is the exact thing I coach people through. I teach them to reach out, to ask for help, not to suffer in silence.

And there I was… suffering in silence. Drowning in it.
Not taking my own damn advice.

There's this pressure—spoken or not—that if you work in the mental health field, you're supposed to have it all figured out. Like we're supposed to be the example. The rock-solid one. The one who doesn't fall apart. The truth is, we're just as human as everyone else.

Human suffering doesn't give a damn about your résumé.
It doesn't care about your degrees, your job title, your bank account, or how many people you've helped along the way.

It will bring you to your knees.
And it did.

If nothing else, I hope I can be a voice for others who are suffering alone. Anyone who feels like they have to hold it all together.

You don't.
You're allowed to fall apart.
You're allowed to be real.
You're allowed to be human.

I'm sorry I didn't let people in.
I'm sorry I did it alone.

But I'm also proud of myself for finally exposing the truth.

But for the love of God…Don't pity me.
Don't call me broken or feel bad for me.

I'm okay now. Like, *really* okay.

For the first time in a long time, I'm not pretending.
I'm not performing.
I'm just here, still standing.

Humbled, human, and healing.

To the version of me who carried it all in silence:

I'm sorry.

I'm sorry for the way I dismissed your pain. I'm sorry for the way I
spoke to you when you were already shattered.
I'm sorry for the times you were barely holding on,
and I told you to be stronger.

For treating your exhaustion like it was a weakness
and your needs like an inconvenience.

You shouldn't have had to be so brave,
so composed,
so alone.

You didn't need to earn rest or love.
You just needed someone to say,
"You're Enough"

And I should've been the one to say it.
I should've protected you.
Listened to you.
Loved you better.

I see you now, in your wholeness.

I love you, Lainey.
I'm sorry.

(No reflection prompt on this one.
This was for *her,* and *she* deserves it..
But if you owe yourself an apology, consider this your moment...)

"I'm sorry" was how I ended my 100 days.
Not just an apology—but a release.
Not just for others, but for me.

It was a moment of truth.
A reckoning between who I was and who I'm becoming.
I made peace with the version of me who held it all together while everything was falling apart.
I apologized for making her carry it alone.
She never deserved that weight—
But she survived.

And I finally told her:
I see you. I'm sorry. You can rest now.

Now It's Your Turn

I've given you my truth, my wisdom shaped by struggle, built through strength, tears, and the choice to show up when disappearing felt safer. Now the next chapter belongs to you.

This is your invitation to rise, to tell your story, and to walk this path with your own grit, grace, and raw, unfiltered honesty.

Healing isn't about becoming someone new.
It's about returning to who you were before the world told you to play it small.

Own your truth.
Make it yours.
Create your own wisdom, and leave your mark.

Because recovery isn't just about getting better—it's about remembering who the Fuck you are!

Reflection Prompt:

You've walked with me through the fire, now it's time to step into your own.

What would it look like to show up for *your* healing with the same raw honesty?

Are you ready to stop reading other people's stories—and start writing your own?

The Beginning

I've never resonated with the word *alcoholic*. Or *addict*.

Maybe because I grew up in a world where drinking wasn't just accepted—it was celebrated. It was the norm, the reward, the escape. It was woven into everything. And for a long time, I didn't know there was another way.

It took years of unraveling.
Countless days of waking up and choosing discomfort over denial.
Years of trying different tools, healing in layers, and learning to trust myself again.

Sobriety isn't my whole identity.
It's part of my story, but it's not the whole damn book.

Because even when I was lost in the toxic loop of numbing and binging, I still accomplished some incredible shit.
And if I could do all that while drowning…
Just wait and see what I can do now: clear, steady, and free.

Now, I'm rising.

This book doesn't close the story.
It opens the door.
The future is unknown, but I've paved a path forward.
I'm not done. Not even close.
There are more lessons ahead. More wisdom to earn.
Another version of me yet to meet.

This isn't the final chapter. This isn't *The End*. It's only *The Beginning*.

To the ones who doubted me, underestimated me, or tried to break me—

F*ck you. Watch me.

www.ingramcontent.com/pod-product-compliance
Lightning Source LLC
Chambersburg PA
CBHW051211120626
46547CB00013B/1299